Simple Machines
at Work

Inclined Planes in Action

Gillian Gosman

Clifton Park - Halfmoon Public Library
475 Moe Road
Clifton Park, New York 12065

PowerKiDS
press™

New York

Published in 2011 by The Rosen Publishing Group, Inc.
29 East 21st Street, New York, NY 10010

First Edition

Editor: Maggie Murphy
Book Design: Kate Laczynski
Photo Researcher: Jessica Gerweck

Photo Credits: Cover, pp. 4, 5, 7, 8, 10, 14, 15 (bottom), 17 Shutterstock.com; back cover and interior cement background graphic © www.iStockphoto.com/walrusmail; back cover and interior graphic (behind some images) © www.iStockphoto.com/Ivan Gusev; p. 9 Chijo Takeda/Getty Images; p. 11 © www.iStockphoto.com/Ben Blankenburg; pp. 12–13 Philip and Karen Smith/Getty Images; p. 15 (top) Hulton Archive/Getty Images; p. 16 Lester Lefkowitz/ Getty Images; p. 18 © www.iStockphoto.com/Ron Bailey; p. 19 (top) Realistic Reflections/Getty Images; p. 19 (bottom) © Dieter Matthes/age fotostock; pp. 20, 21 © Rosen Publishing; p. 22 Brian Bailey/Getty Images.

Library of Congress Cataloging-in-Publication Data

Gosman, Gillian.
  Inclined planes in action / Gillian Gosman.
      p. cm. — (Simple machines at work)
  Includes index.
  ISBN 978-1-4488-0685-0 (library binding) — ISBN 978-1-4488-1303-2 (pbk.) — ISBN 978-1-4488-1304-9 (6-pack)
  1. Inclined planes—Juvenile literature. I. Title.
  TJ147.G678 2011
  621.8'11—dc22
                                    2010003271

Manufactured in the United States of America

CPSIA Compliance Information: Batch #WS10PK: For Further Information contact Rosen Publishing, New York, New York at 1-800-237-9932

What Is an Inclined Plane? 4

The Parts of an Inclined Plane 6

The Inclined Plane's Advantage 8

Inclined Planes at Work 10

Inclined Planes in Nature 12

Inclined Planes Throughout History 14

Inclined Planes on the Job 16

Everyday Inclined Planes 18

An Experiment with an Inclined Plane 20

Smooth Riding 22

Glossary 23

Index 24

Web Sites 24

What Is an Inclined Plane?

This ramp is an inclined plane.

Inclined planes look very simple. However, they can help us do a lot of work with only a little **effort**. An inclined plane is a **surface** with one end raised above the other. The word "inclined" means "raised at one end." An inclined plane is used to move an object from a lower place to a higher place or from a higher place to a lower place. We push the object along the surface of the plane.

The inclined plane is one of six simple machines. A simple machine is an object with few moving parts that helps us do a job. The other simple machines are the pulley, the lever, the wedge, the wheel and axle, and the screw.

This is the Duquesne Incline, an inclined-plane railroad, or funicular, in Pittsburgh, Pennsylvania.

The Parts of an Inclined Plane

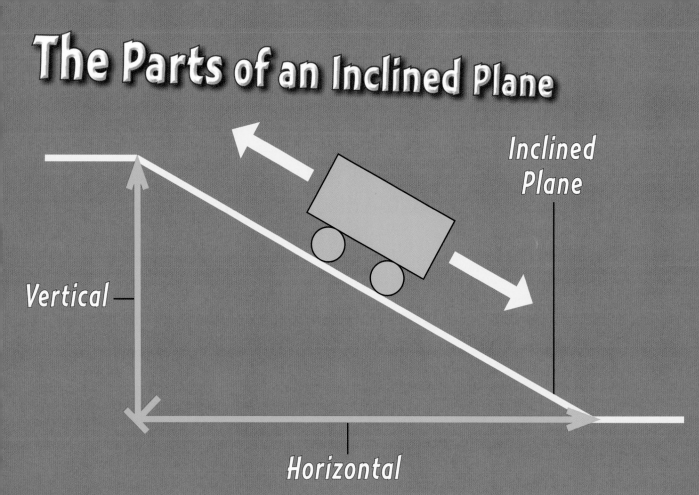

Inclined Plane

Vertical —

Horizontal

The inclined plane has no moving parts. This simple machine is really just a **sloped** surface. It might be made out of metal, concrete, plastic, or wood. It might be **permanent**, such as a road. The inclined plane could also be **temporary**, such as a ramp used to load heavy objects into a truck.

There are three key measurements in an inclined plane. Together, these measurements form an imaginary triangle. People or objects travel along the sloped surface of the inclined plane.

Here, you can see how the measurements of an inclined plane make an imaginary triangle.

These men are using a ramp to help them lift furniture into a truck. The slope of the ramp is less steep than the vertical distance from the top of the ramp to the ground.

This surface rises at an **angle** from the **horizontal**, or the flat base of the triangle. The height the plane covers is the **vertical** distance from the base to the top of the sloped surface.

7

The Inclined Plane's Advantage

A path, like this one, that winds around a mountain until it reaches its top, is really just a long inclined plane.

Imagine yourself standing at the bottom of a tall mountain. Would you rather climb straight up the steep side of the mountain or walk up a winding road that circles the mountain? If you want to save your effort, it would be wise to walk on the road to get to the top.

That winding mountain road is really a long inclined plane. When you move along an inclined plane, you must travel a longer horizontal distance than if you traveled straight up the vertical distance in order to reach the top of the triangle. However,

The slope of this spiral staircase is an example of a very long, coiled inclined plane.

with the inclined plane, you do not need to apply as much effort to do the job. The help you get from the inclined plane is called the machine's mechanical advantage.

Inclined Planes at Work

This boat ramp has a very small angle of incline but a very long sloping surface.

The mechanical advantage of an inclined plane depends on the length of the sloped surface and the amount of vertical distance covered. These measurements tell you the angle of incline, or how steep the sloped surface is. The smaller the angle of incline, the longer the sloped surface and the easier the job will be. However, if the sloped surface is longer, the distance to the top will also be greater. This means that it will take longer to finish the job than if the sloped surface were shorter.

It will take this biker less time to ride up this steep hill than if he took a winding path around it. His ride will be harder, though.

On the other hand, an inclined plane with a greater angle of incline will have a steeper, but shorter, sloped surface. It will take more effort but less time to move across this plane.

Inclined Planes in Nature

No one person **invented** the inclined plane. Rather, inclined planes have always been found in nature. In fact, inclined planes can be seen all over the natural world. Streams and rivers travel downhill, along the sloped paths of hills and

mountains. Mountains are some of the largest inclined planes on Earth.

Animals such as deer, horses, and goats take winding paths up and down the hills and mountains where they live. It takes longer for them to climb up and down these paths than if they were to

Here, bighorn sheep run up a mountain's steep incline.

climb straight up or down the side of the hill or mountain. It takes much less effort, though.

The leaves of a plant can work like an inclined plane, too. They collect, or gather, rainwater and direct it down to the roots of the plant.

13

Many people think that ancient Egyptian pyramids in Giza, Egypt, shown here, were built with the help of inclined planes.

People have used inclined planes throughout history to build temples, **aqueducts**, and roads. Ancient Egyptians used inclined planes made of dirt when they built pyramids. These long ramps were built alongside the pyramids. The large stone blocks used to build the pyramid itself were pushed, pulled, or carted up the ramp.

14

The ancient Romans used inclined planes in war. In 72 CE, the Romans attacked the Jewish fort at Masada, in present-day Israel, for many months. The fort

This drawing shows Roman soldiers pulling a weapon up the ramp they built at Masada.

The ancient Romans likely built this aqueduct in southern France with the help of inclined planes.

sat at the top of a high cliff. In order to reach the top of the cliff and enter the fort without having to climb straight up the cliff, the Romans built a long ramp along the cliff's face.

Inclined Planes on the Job

Here, dirt is being emptied out of the back of a dump truck.

Inclined planes are commonly used in the workplace. Trucks bringing food, furniture, and many other things in large amounts somewhere often have their own temporary ramps. These ramps can be set against the back of the truck to wheel or slide goods in and out. The rear bed of a dump truck also works like an inclined plane when it lifts one end of the bed and dumps out whatever is inside.

Perhaps the smallest inclined plane in the workplace is the **wood screw**. The thread of metal that circles the screw is like the winding road that climbs around a mountain. It cuts through the wood and allows us to screw it in with less effort.

A wood screw's spiral thread, shown here, is a long inclined plane.

Everyday Inclined Planes

You can find wheelchair ramps in many public places.

You likely see and use inclined planes every day. At most street corners, there is a short incline at the curb. In front of your school, a post office, or store, there may be a ramp to the door. These inclined planes make it easier for people with carts, baby

18

There are also temporary ramps that can help people in wheelchairs and motorized scooters get on buses.

strollers, or **wheelchairs** to come and go.

Inclined planes also help people and objects travel down. The walls and bottom of a bathtub and sink are inclined planes that direct the flow of water toward the drain. The angled roof of a house works the same way.

Another ramp you might see is one that helps people carry their bags and suitcases onto a boat.

An Experiment with an Inclined Plane

This **experiment** will help show the mechanical advantage of the inclined plane in moving a heavy object across a vertical distance.

What You Will Need:
- a large rock
- several thick books
- a board or ramp
- string
- a rubber band

step 3

1. Wind the string around the rock, and tie the string to the rubber band.

2. Pile the books, one of top of the other. Begin with the rock resting on the floor by the pile of books.

3. Holding on to the rubber band, lift the rock vertically until it is level with the top book. Notice how much the rubber band is stretching.

4. Now set the ramp against the pile of books, and pull the rock up the ramp. Notice how much the rubber band stretches when you do this.

step 4

5. The longer the rubber band stretches, the more force is needed to lift the rock up to the top of the books. If the rubber band does not need to stretch as much, it means that less force is needed to lift the rock.

Smooth Riding

Inclined planes can be used for many things besides work and war. Many sports use inclined planes, too. Ski hills, ski jumps, and skateboard ramps are all examples of inclined planes. Athletes in the winter sports of luge, skeleton, and bobsled all race

very fast on sleds down icy inclined planes.

At the water park or on the playground, slides are inclined planes that are just for fun. With the help of **gravity**, a slide can help you move very quickly with almost no effort at all!

Glossary

angle (ANG-gul) The space between two lines or planes that come together at a point.

aqueducts (A-kweh-dukts) Pipes used to carry water for long distances.

effort (EH-fert) The amount of force applied to an object.

experiment (ik-SPER-uh-ment) A set of actions or steps taken to learn more about something.

gravity (GRA-vih-tee) The natural force that causes objects to move toward the center of Earth.

horizontal (hor-ih-ZON-til) Going from side to side.

invented (in-VENT-ed) Made something new.

permanent (PER-muh-nint) Lasting for a long time.

sloped (SLOHPD) At an angle.

surface (SER-fes) The outside of anything.

temporary (TEM-puh-rer-ee) Lasting for a short amount of time.

vertical (VER-tih-kul) In an up-and-down direction.

wheelchairs (WEEL-cherz) Chairs on wheels that are used by people who cannot walk.

wood screw (WUHD SKROO) A screw with a slotted head and a pointed end.

Index

A
angle, 7, 10–11

C
concrete, 6

E
effort, 4, 8–9, 11, 13, 17, 22

G
gravity, 22

H
height, 7
horizontal, 7, 9

J
job, 5, 9, 11

L
lever, 5

M
mechanical advantage, 9–10, 20
metal, 6, 17

P
parts, 5–6
people, 7, 12, 14, 18–19
plastic, 6
pulley, 5

R
ramp(s), 6, 14–16, 18, 20–22
road(s), 6, 8–9, 14, 17

S
surface, 4–7, 10–11

W
wedge, 5
wheel and axle, 5
wheelchairs, 19
wood, 6
wood screw, 17
work, 4, 22

Due to the changing nature of Internet links, PowerKids Press has developed an online list of Web sites related to the subject of this book. This site is updated regularly. Please use this link to access the list:

www.powerkidslinks.com/sm/ip/

24